WORKING WITH HUMANS
WORKBOOK

WORKING WITH HUMANS

WORKBOOK

Tools You Didn't Know You Needed for
Conversations You Never Expected to Have

LAURA CRANDALL

BANQUET
PUBLISHING

Copyright © 2024 by Laura Crandall

All rights reserved. No part of this publication may be reproduced, stored in a retrieval system, or transmitted in any form or by any means, without prior permission in writing from the publisher. This includes use in any manner for purposes of training artificial intelligence technologies to generate text, including without limitation, technologies that are capable of generating works in the same style or genre as this publication.

Library of Congress Control Number: 2024919846

ISBN: 979-8-9882254-4-7

Cover and text design by Alex Hennig
Map illustration by Stef Koehler
Interior illustrations by Molly Russell

Banquet Publishing

Belmont, MA, USA
banquetpublishing.com

Contents

Welcome!   **1**

The Essential Tools

Essential Tool #1:
Your Character Compass   **5**

Essential Tool #2:
The Communication Must-Haves   **17**

Essential Tool #3:
The Key Behaviors   **33**

Next Steps   **39**

Navigating Your Way

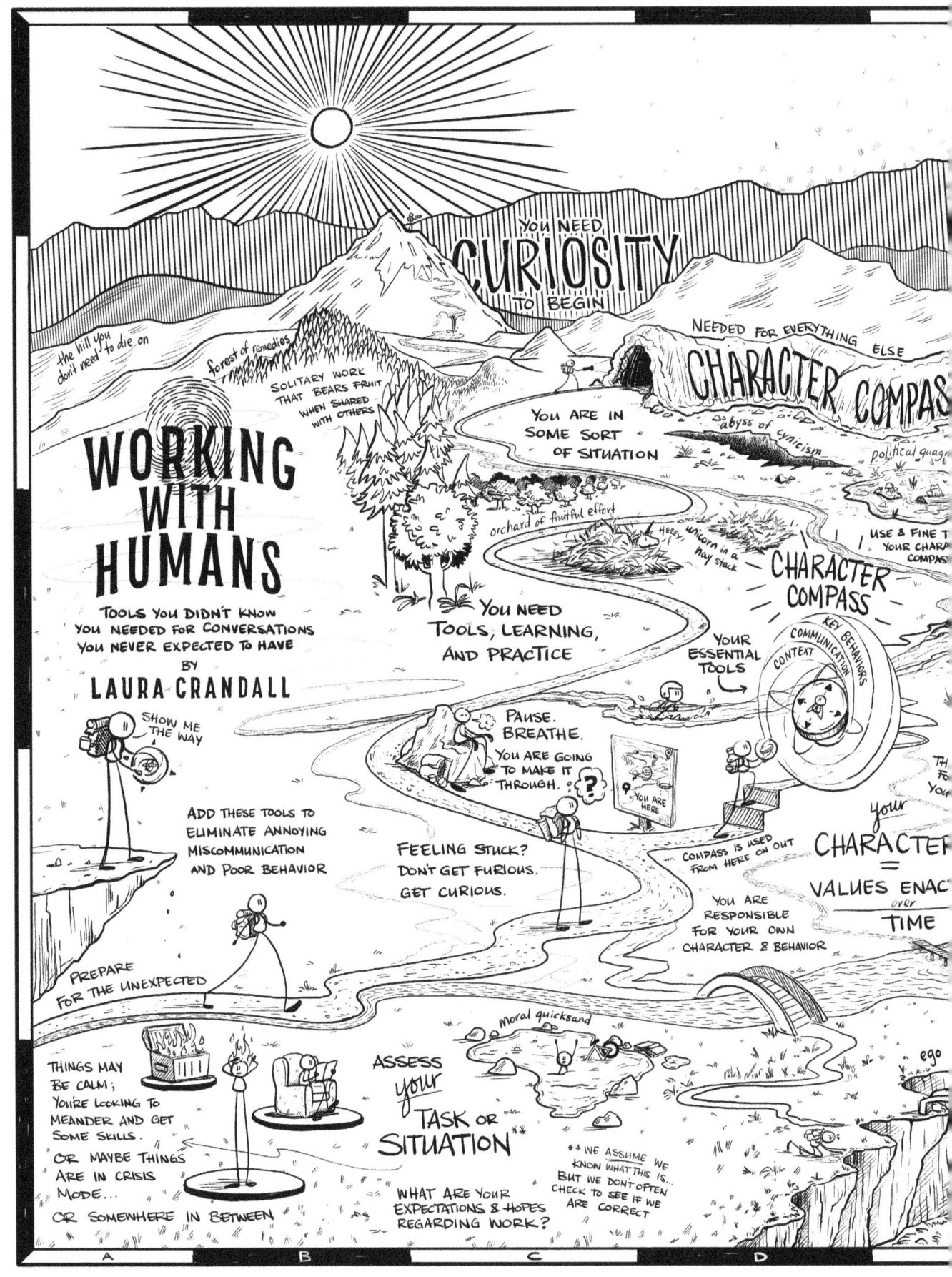

The landscape of Working With Humans is varied and rich. There are beautiful opportunities and splendid vistas as well as tricky situations and spots to avoid. When you set out to build your skills and knowledge and then share your experiences with others, it makes for a wonderful adventure.

Welcome!

Now is a great time to become good at working with humans.

You have in your hands the workbook of supporting materials and exercises from *Working With Humans: Tools You Didn't Know You Needed for Conversations You Never Expected To Have*. This is a place to reflect on the questions posed in the book and sort through your thoughts and ideas. It's also a handy space for writing things down. Behold: the power of 8.5"x11"-inch pages!

The exercises here are the same that are referenced in the book and audiobook and follow the same sequence mentioned in the text. Go forth and play with these exercises. Each one is intended to help you get to know how your own humanity can help you (and the people around you) get better at working with humans.

Your First Assignment: How Do You Want to Feel at Work?

When we set out to fix a problem at work, all of our attention goes toward getting the problem to stop. We find a solution, apply it to that immediate situation, and move on. A short time later, when a similar problem pops up, we have a way to fix it: just apply our recent solution again. And again. And before we know it, we're playing Whack-a-Mole with workplace irritants.

We get stuck in this solution loop because we forget to think about what success looks like *beyond* fixing the problem. What will that successful state feel like, and how will we recognize it when it happens? Note the word *feel*. Thinking is important, but for this assignment, focus on feeling. Knowing how you feel—in your body, heart, and spirit—is part of bringing humanity back into work, so that's where we'll start.

Read the following questions and let your mind wander a bit. Your responses may be short and succinct, or you may write paragraphs. Either is fine.

Recognize When Working With Humans Is **Working.**

Your responses should be specific enough that you notice how you feel, even if no one else does.

Take a few easy, slow breaths and let your mind relax. Then write down your answers.*

---

* *Try writing your responses by hand with pen and paper. Noticing how it feels to physically write is another way to bring your body into this activity.*

1. When I learn to communicate well, even in unexpected circumstances at work:

   - I will feel...
     Examples: hopeful, more confident, less intimidated by Veronica in Accounts Payable

   - I will notice that I feel this way when I...
     Examples: spend less time worrying about a conversation I had with my boss, am able to be clear with direction and timelines for my team, can talk calmly with Veronica when I spot an error on her weekly reports

2. When my coworkers and people I manage are doing better because communication and behavior have improved all around:

   - I will feel...
     Examples: like we can be more effective as a team, that we like each other

   - I will notice this is happening when...
     Examples: daily snarkiness decreases, people laugh more, I don't feel like I hate everyone I work with

3. Dream come true, at the end of a good day at work:

   - I will feel...

   - When this happens, I will notice it because...
     Examples: I will feel like I'm happier with my job because work is done without as much strain and nonsense. I will feel more at ease when I talk about my work with my friends and family.

After you've answered these questions, go for a walk or gaze up at the stars or lift weights or knit—something you enjoy that is not work-related. Then come back to your answers to see if they need modification or clarification. Adjust as needed. Keep these answers close. You'll come back to them later.

It may seem strange to daydream about answers to the questions above. It may feel precarious to be hopeful about what's possible. But without that vision of the future, that hope, we won't get very far. Hope is a form of planning. It's the beginning of the structure of how we create change. Your hope and your vision are vital. Now, let's learn the tools that can make them real.

The Essential Tools

Everything that makes working with humans more effective revolves around three Essential Tools. They are like a decoder ring, magic wand, and your most comfortable pair of shoes all rolled into one: they will help you understand your colleagues, transform interactions for the better, and give you a confident spring in your step. The Essential Tools will keep you grounded, focused, and calm as you work with humans.

They are:

_____

1. **Your Character Compass**
2. **The Communication Must-Haves**
3. **The Key Behaviors**

_____

The exercises and assignments that follow ask you to explore your own relationship with each of the Essential Tools. Please reference the text or audiobook for deeper context and discussion of each of these essential, powerful, and delightfully handy tools.

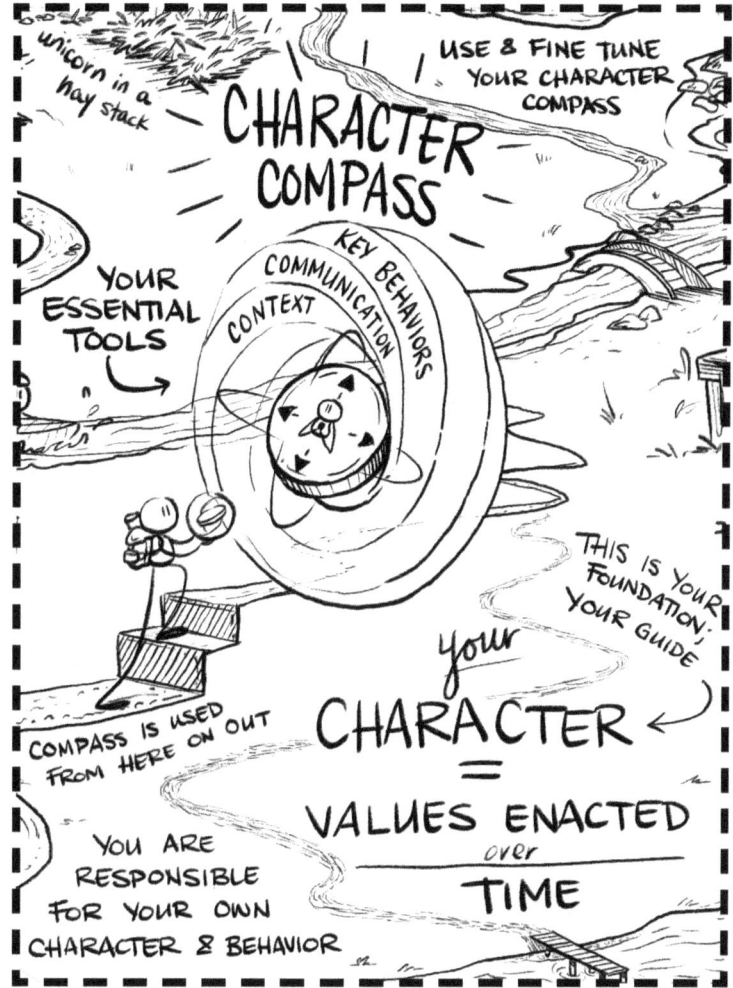

Essential Tool #1: Your Character Compass

Moral philosophers would describe character with greater detail and nuance, but in general terms: character is developed by enacting your values consistently, over time. Character builds on itself. The more you work on it, the more resilient it can become.

Character Compass | Step One:

Below is a long list of qualities that contribute to creating character. Circle the ten that are most meaningful to you. These can be qualities you value in yourself, that are inspired by others, or some combination of both. We all use all of these qualities, so circle the ones that resonate most for you.

Accomplishment	Courtesy	Humor	Perseverance	Spirituality
Accountability	Creativity	Imagination	Persistence	Stability
Adaptability	Curiosity	Independence	Playfulness	Status
Altruism	Decisiveness	Individuality	Poise	Stewardship
Ambition	Dependability	Insight	Potential	Strength
Assertiveness	Determination	Integrity	Power	Structure
Attentiveness	Devotion	Intelligence	Presence	Success
Awareness	Dignity	Intuition	Prosperity	Support
Balance	Discipline	Irreverence	Purpose	Sustainability
Beauty	Effectiveness	Joy	Quality	Teamwork
Boldness	Empathy	Justice	Reason	Temperance
Bravery	Endurance	Kindness	Recognition	Tenacity
Brilliance	Energy	Knowledge	Recreation	Thankfulness
Calmness	Enthusiasm	Lawfulness	Respect	Thoroughness
Certainty	Excellence	Leadership	Responsibility	Thoughtfulness
Charity	Experience	Learning	Reverence	Tolerance
Clarity	Fairness	Liberty	Rigor	Trust
Cleverness	Fidelity	Logic	Risk	Truthfulness
Commitment	Foresight	Love	Security	Understanding
Common sense	Fortitude	Loyalty	Self-reliance	Uniqueness
Communication	Friendship	Mastery	Selflessness	Unity
Community	Fun	Meaning	Sensitivity	Valor
Compassion	Generosity	Moderation	Serenity	Vigor
Competence	Grace	Motivation	Service	Vision
Confidence	Gratitude	Openness	Sharing	Vitality
Connection	Growth	Optimism	Significance	Wisdom
Consistency	Happiness	Order	Simplicity	Wonder
Contentment	Honesty	Originality	Sincerity	
Conviction	Honor	Passion	Skillfulness	
Cooperation	Hope	Patience	Smarts	
Courage	Humility	Peace	Solitude	

Additional qualities:

Character Compass | Step Two:

Look at the ten qualities you circled that contribute to character. Are some more important than others? Do some of them build off each other or offer sharp contrast to each other? Bring some curiosity to the values and behaviors you find meaningful in your own life and reflect on the ways each one influences your choices and actions during the differing circumstances of daily life.

Prioritize your list in the space below. Is there one quality that is most important to you? Are there a few that are the key drivers in your life? A few that you'd like to emphasize more? Write them down and then see which of them keep drawing your attention.

1	6
2	7
3	8
4	9
5	10

TOP 4

Character Compass | Step Three:

From your list of ten, choose the four qualities that are the most important to YOU. They may be different from what other people or influences in your life expect them to be. These are the qualities you feel most drawn to in EVERY situation: personal, professional, social, financial, etc. (Why only four? It makes remembering them easier!)

These qualities of character are now your compass headings—your touchstones for navigating the world and how you work with humans.

This compass is a tool to help you make values-informed choices and develop the character you want to have as you navigate the world and your experiences within it.

When you make choices, ask yourself if they align with your compass headings. If they do, carry on. If they don't, ask yourself: why not? They may be misaligned with your values. Making choices that are rooted in your character makes working with humans easier.

The words you listed as your top ten and the ones you chose for your Character Compass points are important to you and, hopefully, are good for you, too. But there can be too much or too little of a good thing. Aristotle (384-322 BCE) believed that character could be developed with effort and attention. His table of virtues and vices shows how even the best qualities of character can be problematic in their extreme forms. He strove for the mean, the middle balance, where each quality works and feels best.

As you continue to practice with your Character Compass, look to see if any of your chosen qualities align with the mean, below. These are qualities that many people associate with character, even when they use complementary words to describe them. Being able to recognize where your values connect to, complement, or contrast with the values of others can be a handy anchor for better conversation as you work with humans.

Remember: Character is developed by enacting your values consistently, over time.

Aristotle's Table of Virtues and Vices:

SPHERE OF ACTION OR FEELING	EXCESS	MEAN	DEFICIENCY
Fear and Confidence	Rashness	**Courage**	Cowardice
Pleasure and Pain	Licentiousness/Self-indulgence	**Temperance**	Insensibility
Getting and Spending (minor)	Prodigality	**Liberality**	Illiberality/Meanness
Getting and Spending (major)	Vulgarity/Tastelessness	**Magnificence**	Pettiness/Stinginess
Honor and Dishonor (major)	Vanity	**Magnanimity**	Pusillanimity
Honor and Dishonor (minor)	Ambition/Empty vanity	**Proper ambition/Pride**	Unambitiousness/Undue humility
Anger	Irascibility	**Patience/Good temper**	Lack of spirit/Unirascibility
Self-expression	Boastfulness	**Truthfulness**	Understatement/Mock modesty
Conversation	Buffoonery	**Wittiness**	Boorishness
Social Conduct	Obsequiousness	**Friendliness**	Cantankerousness
Shame	Shyness	**Modesty**	Shamelessness
Indignation	Envy	**Righteous indignation**	Malicious enjoyment/Spitefulness

Aristotle. The Ethics of Aristotle: The Nicomachean Ethics. (rev. ed.) (J. K. Thomson, trans.). New York: Viking, 1955.

Practice With a Pal: Character

Practice, practice, practice

1. **Find a pal at work.** *A pal is someone worthy of your trust, open to direct and meaningful discussion of topics, and who supports your learning and development as a person.* If you don't have a pal at work, that's a bummer, but it's okay. Just find a person in your life who is open to talking about things other than the weather (heck, strike up a conversation on the bus or with your postal carrier if that feels easier).

   - Tell your pal that you are working on developing your communication skills and need their help. You want to talk about the qualities of character most of us take for granted in day-to-day life.

   They may look a little surprised because it's not a common topic of conversation—fear not! We need to make these conversations normal if we are going to acknowledge the humanity in our workplaces.

2. **Set aside some time**—ten to twenty minutes—to talk about the qualities of character you find most meaningful.

   - Before you meet, reflect on your own Character Compass headings *(Use the worksheets on pages 12-15)*.

   Pick one and start the conversation with these questions:

     » *What's your definition of /what comes to mind when you think of this quality?*
     » *How do you notice it in others? What are they doing that demonstrates this quality?*
     » *For extra fun: have your friend draw an image of this quality in action.*
     » *When do you see this at work?*

   Listen to your pal's answers and then ask them to listen as you answer the same questions.

   - Then, discuss your answers:
     » *How are your answers similar?*
     » *How are they different?*
     » *Do your responses complement each other? Contradict? Do they provide a more well-rounded definition of the quality? Do they help you know your pal better?*

- Do this for the other values on your Character Compass.

- This discussion allows you to understand each other more fully and to talk about a topic—values—in a neutral way that brings open-hearted curiosity into the conversation.

3. **If you're up for it,** here are a couple of questions to continue the conversation:
    » *What's the one quality of character you want to be known for, and why?*

    » *Who are your heroes, and why?*

With each of these questions and answers, listen deeply. Your replies and definitions will both contrast and complement each other. The point is to start practicing the discussion of values and qualities of character.

Bonus Activity:
These are the kind of conversations we need to be having about politics. Can you bring your character with you into a topic where you and your pal have different political perspectives? If you orient yourself to the conversation using your Character Compass before you begin, what happens as you talk? Can you listen differently? Can you hear the values the other person is trying to describe when they express a difference?

Even if you cannot discuss politics with people who think and feel differently than you do, you can listen and identify the values and qualities of character that are important in someone else's opinion. We must find the courage to recognize and make use of the qualities we share if we are to salvage our communities and national landscape from the perils of polarization.

Pre-Practice With a Pal Reflection:

Character Compass Value: _____

What's your definition of /what comes to mind when you think of this quality?

How do you notice it in others? What are they doing that demonstrates this quality?

When do you see this at work?

Discuss your answers:
- How are your answers similar?
- How are they different?
- Do your responses complement each other? Contradict? Do they provide a more well-rounded definition of the quality? Do they help you know your pal better?

Post-Practice Reflection/Notes:

Pre-Practice With a Pal Reflection:

Character Compass Value: _____

What's your definition of /what comes to mind when you think of this quality?

How do you notice it in others? What are they doing that demonstrates this quality?

When do you see this at work?

Discuss your answers:
- How are your answers similar?
- How are they different?
- Do your responses complement each other? Contradict? Do they provide a more well-rounded definition of the quality? Do they help you know your pal better?

Post-Practice Reflection/Notes:

Pre-Practice With a Pal Reflection:

Character Compass Value: _____

What's your definition of /what comes to mind when you think of this quality?

How do you notice it in others? What are they doing that demonstrates this quality?

When do you see this at work?

Discuss your answers:
- How are your answers similar?
- How are they different?
- Do your responses complement each other? Contradict? Do they provide a more well-rounded definition of the quality? Do they help you know your pal better?

Post-Practice Reflection/Notes:

Pre-Practice With a Pal Reflection:

Character Compass Value: _____

What's your definition of /what comes to mind when you think of this quality?

How do you notice it in others? What are they doing that demonstrates this quality?

When do you see this at work?

Discuss your answers:
- How are your answers similar?
- How are they different?
- Do your responses complement each other? Contradict? Do they provide a more well-rounded definition of the quality? Do they help you know your pal better?

Post-Practice Reflection/Notes:

Essential Tool #2: The Communication Must-Haves

How many times have you had a conversation where you thought you knew what you'd agreed upon, only to have the other person do something else entirely? Or nothing at all?

Miscommunication and misunderstanding are the sources of irritations in the workplace, ranging from client contract disputes to people being perpetually late to meetings to whether the heating and cooling system works. 99% of all problems at work are because of problems in our communication.

The Communication Must Haves are made of two different tools that will help you hone your communication skills by focusing on your ability to ask good questions, listen to answers and information with better clarity, and build trust and shared understanding about the hopes and expectations that go into every conversation at work.

The worksheets on the following pages explore the **Core Questions** and **The Four Things To Do Forever**. You'll also get to look at your own expectations about communication and behaviors at work with **The Expectations Inventory**. Consider working on these next three exercises with your Character Compass at hand.

Core Questions – Worksheet

What do you want to talk about? What's your topic? Keep that in mind as you ask and answer each of the four Core Questions. A little bit of reflection to organize your ideas before a conversation can help you prepare for the unexpected and connect more effectively with others.

You can start by asking yourself any of these questions, but make sure you ask and answer all in preparation for sharing information with others. Keep asking good questions and notice how each one can support the clarity of the others. **Use the squares below to answer each of the Core Questions as they pertain to the topic you want to discuss.**

*IF everyone uses this information or skill well, what will happen? What's the **VISION** for the future? What do you hope will happen? How might this information be applied elsewhere?*

*This question gives background and **CONTEXT** to the information. It engages others with examples and experiences they can relate to and care about. WHY helps you share why the topic is relevant and important.*

★ *It's often handiest to ask WHY first – then you know why you care, too.*

*This is where people get to put new information into **ACTION**. This is where everyone (including you) gets to practice and experiment with HOW ideas and next steps can work.*

*This is the **DATA** and the expertise behind it. WHAT is made of the specific list of details people need to know to be effective in using new information.*

Source: Adapted from About Learning and 4MAT4Business

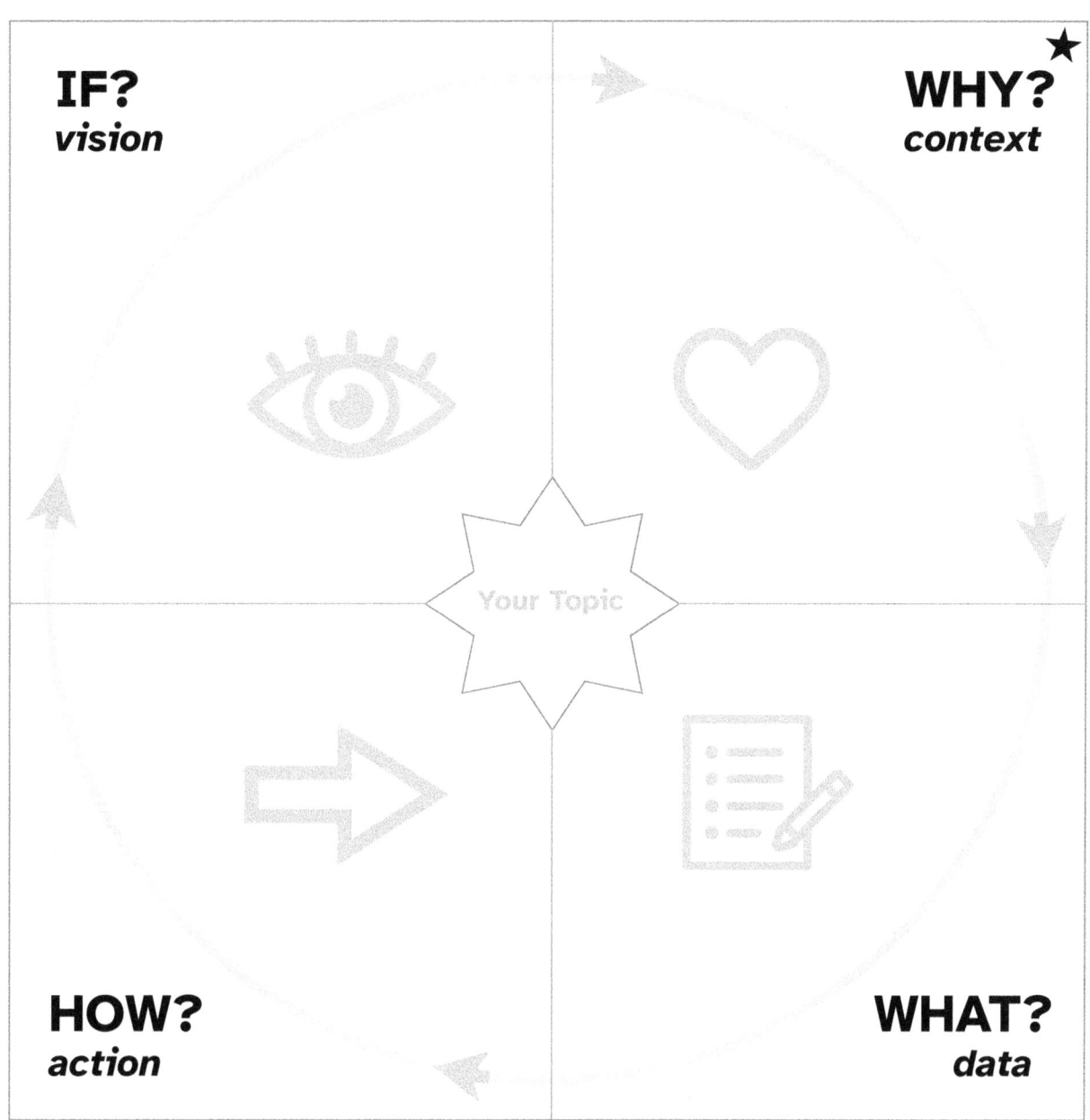

Four Things to Do Forever—
Let's Get Clear

Think of a time when you became frustrated, fed-up, or disappointed because someone didn't do what you expected them to. A key data point didn't make it into a slide deck, a client wasn't called when scheduled, someone didn't check for dietary restrictions and the ten vegans at your lunch event got seriously hangry while staring at a pile of turkey sandwiches. Whatever the situation, grab a piece of paper, and write down what you expected or hoped would happen. Then write down what actually happened.

Disappointing Situation

What I Expected to Happen:

What Actually Happened:

Now think about a time when a conversation or plan went well. What was the circumstance? How did you feel when you realized that everything was going smoothly? What did you say to your coworkers after things ended well? Maybe you were expecting that a colleague would disagree with your recommendation, but as you took the time to discuss the situation, you found out you both wanted the same thing. Whatever your experience, write it down.

Satisfying Situation

What I Expected to Happen:

What Actually Happened:

These contrasting experiences will be your reference point as we dive into the second communication tool to make working with humans easier: the Four Things to Do Forever.

The Four Things to Do Forever are incredibly helpful in a fantastically boring way: if you practice these four things in every conversation that involves a next step and repeat them forever—and I mean FOR-*EV*-ER—your communication will become clearer, more effective, more inclusive, and lend itself to better results and relationships. Those outcomes make the boring nature of this tool totally worthwhile.

The Four Things to Do Forever are:

1. **Communicate Clearly**
2. **Establish Expectations**
3. **Get Commitment**
4. **Follow Through**

These four things are what you need to do to ensure that you and your team have a shared understanding of the context, expectations, agreements, and timelines for your work.

The trickiest part of the Four Things To Do Forever is often the second thing: Establish Expectations. Start by examining what you bring to the conversation by doing the **Expectations Inventory.**

Expectations Inventory

Use the chart below to think about the behavioral expectations you have at work. Very often, there are details within our expectations that we don't even know or think about until we take the time to look. Do the following:

1. List the top three behaviors you find frustrating in other people at work (frustrations can be a shortcut to identifying your expectations).
2. Write down a specific example of when you have been frustrated by that behavior.
3. Describe what you assumed or hoped would happen instead.
4. Examine what you hoped would happen. What are the underlying qualities of character that you expect to see enacted? (These are important points for future discussions.)

Read the example below then start to inventory your expectations on the page that follows.

Frustrating Behavior		*People who interrupt and talk over the ideas and input of others meetings.*
Specific Example		*In our team's weekly check-ins, two senior members routinely talk over junior staff and dismiss their questions.*
Behavior I Expected	What I had assumed would happen	• *I expect better manners.* • *I expect people to be attentive to each other's contributions.* • *I expect a meeting facilitator to intervene.*
	Underlying Expectation	• *Inclusion – all people present can contribute* • *Structure – that there is order to meetings* • *Courtesy – toward all participants*

Expectations Inventory: Worksheet

Top 3 Frustrating Behaviors	1
	2
	3

Frustrating Behavior #1	
Specific Example	
Behavior I Expected — What I had assumed would happen	
Behavior I Expected — **Underlying Expectation**	

Frustrating Behavior #2	
Specific Example	

Behavior I Expected	What I had assumed would happen	
	Underlying Expectation	

Frustrating Behavior #3	
Specific Example	

Behavior I Expected	What I had assumed would happen	
	Underlying Expectation	

Now, look at the expectations you identified on the previous page. In the space below, pick one and explore how you came to expect this behaviors in the workplace. Then start to examine why these are important to you and whether others know about and can meet this expectation*. Examining your expectations is an essential part of being able to communicate well.

Underlying Expectation	*Courtesy*
When did I learn it and from whom?	*I learned it from my granddad when I was a little kid.*
Why is it important to me?	*I know it's useful to build and maintain relationships at work; I like knowing I'm using what I learned from my granddad.*
Do other people know I have this expectation?	*Yes (they know, right…? doesn't everyone expect this?)*
Have I talked directly about this expectation?	*I think so, but the conversation could be clarified.*

Underlying Expectation	
When did I learn it and from whom?	
Why is it important to me?	
Do other people know I have this expectation?	
Have I talked directly about this expectation?	

*** A note about expectations**: "High standards" can be good, but if your standards are never met, it can be a signal to explore the expectations that created those standards. Examining who always or never meets your expectations can be a good place to start uncovering implicit cultural biases.

The Four Things To Do Forever are simple in concept, but that doesn't mean they are easy. Each thing has some nuance that is worth diving into. Please see pages 68-87 in *Working With Humans* for the deeper discussion. As you do the following worksheet, keep this short summary in mind:

1. Communicate Clearly

This first step is about you. You are the person who is in charge of what you say when you communicate. You must begin the Four Things with yourself and your awareness of the topic at hand: what you want people to know.

To communicate clearly, start by asking yourself a few background questions:
- What is the purpose or goal of this conversation?
- Why do I care about it?
- What do I need to say?
- What do I hope will happen?
- How will I know if it works?

The answers to these questions help you clarify and refine your thinking and build confidence in what you want to say.

2. Establish Expectations

Most of us don't have a clear idea of what our expectations are until someone lets us down.

When people don't do something in the way we had hoped or envisioned, it's easy to think that other people don't know what they are doing or don't care as much as you do. That may be the case, but it's more likely that you had differing expectations that were unspoken and assumed to be the same.

Tacit expectations are a recipe for disaster. Open, discussed, and agreed upon expectations are an important key to better interactions and successes at work.

3. Get Commitment

Getting commitment is about verifying if someone will or will not do something: yes or no. When communication is clear and expectations are established, either answer is fine. When you ask for an answer that is either yes or no, listen to the response. Yes is great, but no is okay, too. No, in daily conversations, can yield, "Why not? Say more." Nos can build better clarity and cultivate responsibility and solutions that you didn't know were there.

Asking for commitment is a simple point of agreement for a next step and is powerful when done with clarity, curiosity, and character.

4. Follow Through

This step is elegant and intentional. It's also wonderful because it's not all on you: it is shared between you and the person you're communicating with. Once you Get Commitment, you establish a check-in point with the person who has committed to the expectation. It's a way to close the loop and complete things with confidence and ease. All you do is make note of the agreed-upon deadlines or commitments, then follow through to check on progress. Responsibility doesn't have to rest solely with you—the person making the commitment can be responsible for checking in. It's like having someone else help you with your to-do list.

The whole process of the Four Things To Do Forever This whole process is about building a flow of communication around expectations and commitments with other humans at work.

Four Things to Do Forever: Worksheet

For Clearer, More Effective Communication

Topic:

1. Communicate Clearly	*Ask yourself: Why is this conversation important? What do I hope will be the result?*
2. Establish Expectations	*Ask yourself: What do I expect? Are these shared expectations? How do I know they are shared? Do I know the other person's expectations? Clarifying expectations is vital to success.*
3. Get Commitment	*This is a perfect place for a close-ended question! If the answer is no, stay curious and discover Why. Refine and discover what will work until everyone says yes. (Beware of answers like, "I get it" or "I hear you loud and clear." Those are positive statements that are not necessarily, "YES.")*
4. Follow Through	*DO NOT FORGET THIS STEP. It's where trust and confidence are built.*

Practice With a Pal:
Communication Must-Haves

What are the questions you hope no one asks you at your work? Is there a topic you think everyone else knows well but you don't understand? What about things like the history of how your organization was founded or the reason behind that change in health insurance carrier? We all have things that we're supposed to know because they are part of our job, but time-pressure and the sheer volume of stuff we have to know can make deep knowledge of all the details difficult.

Complete the following (and have your pal do the same):

- At work, these are the topics I fake my way through when asked:

- These are the topics I talk around or only give surface-level answers to because I don't feel like an expert:

- I admire _____'s knowledge about _____
  that I listed above.

  One thing I would like to learn from them is:

After you fill out the lists above, pick one topic you'd like to feel more confident in and learn a bit about it.

Chosen Topic:

Then use the Core Questions to describe:

- **Why** you care about this. Share the context or larger background.

- **What** the details are and who you would ask for further information and data.

- **How** you will practice using this information and what you will do with it.

- **If** you learn about this topic you will feel _____.

Then apply the **Four Things to Do Forever**. You can use the same topic you've reflected on above or pick a topic or task that needs to be discussed within your team. For practice, draft answers to the following, and then test them out in an additional conversation with your pal.

1. Communicate Clearly

   State the subject and why it is important (this builds off the Core Questions).

2. Establish Expectations

   Do not make assumptions. "The expectation about this is _____."

3. Get Commitment

   "Will you do it?" is a yes/no question

4. Follow Through

   Put it on the calendar and find out if it's done.

Meet with your pal and share your lists, what you discovered about your topic, how you'd communicate the new information, and which points feel solid or shaky. All of this takes a little deliberate practice. Go forth and be curious and clear!

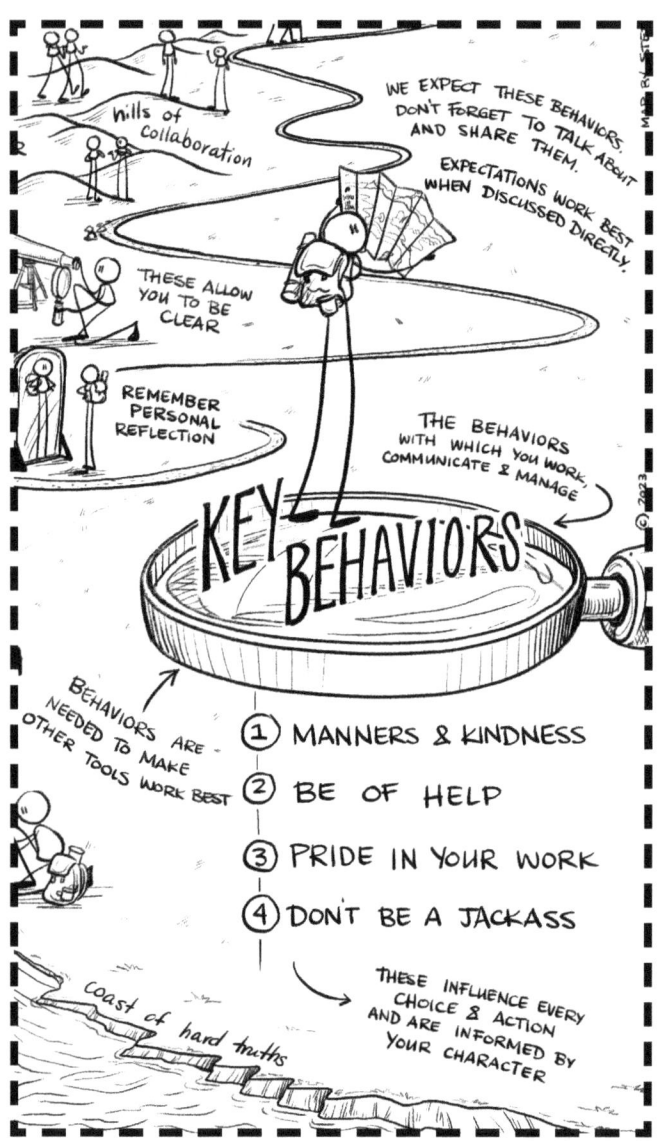

Essential Tool #3: The Key Behaviors

The Key Behaviors are the fundamental actions and attitudes that we expect of each other at work. They consist of three things we expect people to do and one thing we expect people to avoid at all costs. We are generally taught these things when we are young by our families, our religious communities, in early education, or in a social setting like daycare, team sports, or other group activities. As kids, we learn these behaviors early because they help create tolerance, care, and productive cooperation in any setting: they make group dynamics—and, later, work dynamics—easier.

You'd think if something was this helpful to kids at an early age, we'd keep using it throughout our lives, right? Nope. Talking about expected behaviors and attitudes on purpose? That's for kids! How patronizing and demeaning!

Sure, if you talk about these behaviors with a thirty-, sixty-, or ninety- year-old as though they haven't ever heard of them before and don't understand their importance, that would be insulting. But the fundamental skills we teach our kids about working cooperatively are the same behaviors we need from each other at work and in society at large.

The four Key Behaviors are vital to making working with humans easier and better. Why? They are the unspoken expectations that we take for granted and don't know how to talk about until they are messed with—kind of like oxygen: we need it to breathe and don't notice it unless it's a little thin.

The Key Behaviors are:

---

1. Share Manners and Kindness
2. Be of Help
3. Have Pride in Your Work
4. Don't Be a Jackass

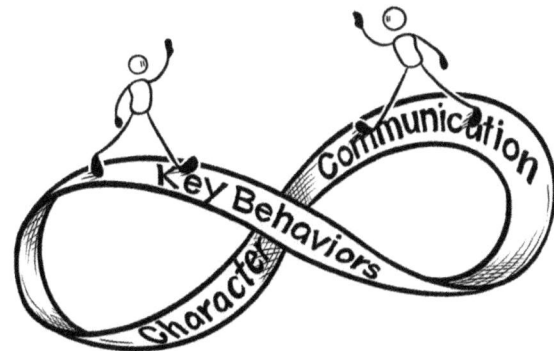

Please refer to the main text or audio of *Working With Humans* for a deeper discussion of the Key Behaviors. To examine how many organizations ask for these behaviors, take a look at the following chart. The behaviors we want from each other at work can be thought of as one of the first three on the Key Behaviors list.

Behaviors Employers Advertise For

Manners and Kindness	Be of Help	Pride in Your Work
Assertive	*Assertive*	**Assertive**
Thorough	Thorough	**Thorough**
Friendly	Friendly	*Friendly*
Prompt and responsive	**Prompt and responsive**	Prompt and responsive
Dynamic	*Dynamic*	*Dynamic*
Open to a flexible work schedule	**Open to a flexible work schedule**	*Open to a flexible work schedule*
Attentive to details	Attentive to details	**Attentive to details**
Able to own and resolve problems	**Able to own and resolve problems**	Able to own and resolve problems
Reliable	**Reliable**	**Reliable**
Service-minded	**Service-minded**	*Service-minded*
Self-directed	Self-directed	**Self-directed**
Results-oriented	Results-oriented	**Results-oriented**
Team player	**Team player**	Team player
Mature	**Mature**	**Mature**
Credible	**Credible**	**Credible**
Excellent communicator	Excellent communicator	**Excellent communicator**

Level of daily emphasis: **High** • Medium • *Low*

About the fourth Key Behavior: Don't Be a Jackass

Jackass (noun): a person who chooses to engage in any manner of behaviors that are rude, obtuse, harmful, corrupt, or obnoxious.

BIG IMPORTANT NOTE: *This last Key Behavior is the most important*. It's the one that I mentioned at the start as the behavior we need **not** to do. It's meant to be a helpful hint, not a punitive scold. "Don't be a jackass" is usually uttered with a fair amount of force and venom. That's *not* the tone here. Imagine it as part of the reminders you may hear or say when leaving the house: *remember your wallet ...have a nice day ...don't be a jackass* ...The stuff that helps us get through the day. Please remember that a joyful, open-hearted laugh is the shortest distance between people.

The statement "Don't Be a Jackass" is meant as a reality check. Jackassedness is a type of behavior—the combined manifestation of an absence of curiosity, a shortage of empathy, and a profound disinterest in anything other than one's own immediate experience. Reminding yourself not to be a jackass helps you evaluate your actions when you feel the pull toward the grim combination of behaviors interrupting people when they speak, using positional power as an excuse for condescension, ignoring the people who helped you along your path once they are no longer of use) that perpetuate the all-too-common workplace routines of self-absorption and neglect of the greater good.

Calmness and curiosity are the natural foes of jackass behavior.

While Don't Be a Jackass is the last of the four Key Behaviors, if you think you can skip it, it's likely that you aren't doing the first three very well. Each of these ideas supports each other, just as each of the Essential Tools intertwine.

As you work on the Practice with a Pal exercise for the Key Behaviors, remember to think about the questions while using your Character Compass and the Communication Must-Haves as tools that help you bring your humanity into each question.

Practice With a Pal:
The Key Behaviors

When you start a new project or work with a new team, talk about the Key Behaviors with everyone. Look back to your First Assignment and to your Expectations Inventory. You can use that structure to frame the conversation and set expectations about shared behaviors. If you create and discuss expectations at the beginning of a project, you create a point of reference that you can refer to if jackassery shows up.

> **Talking about behaviors before they become annoying or problematic is its own diabolically unexpected and fabulous way to bring humanity into working with humans.**

You can practice with a pal, or, if you're feeling like you want to jump in and go for it, practice in a kick-off meeting, a weekly meeting, or even on a Monday-morning huddle.

Start by asking any of the following questions—or add your own!

1. **"As we work on this project, in what ways can we offer help to each other?"**
    - How do we want to acknowledge helpfulness when it happens?
        » *"I noticed that Andrea stepped in and helped to make sure the new addendum was added to the quarterly report in time to send it to the review board. Your work reduced everyone's stress load. Thank you, Andrea."*

2. **"What does doing a good job on this project look like?"**

    - What will you be most proud of when this project is done?
        » *"The project has been going on for what feels like eons and compromising quality would have been easy. The fact that everyone has shown pride in the quality of our work at every step means everything to the integrity of our brand."*

    - Are there temptations to cut corners? What corners specifically?
        » *"We could have shipped all those samples... the color was so close to being right. I'm glad we redid them–the client was amazed with how they looked!"*

3. **"What's the kindest thing that you've noticed people doing for each other lately?"** *

    - What are the little things that we do for each other that you really appreciate?
        » *"Julie, you know I get overwhelmed at the start of new projects and you always send a text to say you believe in me. Your encouragement gets me through my initial jitters. Thank you!"*
        » *"Thanks for holding the door. It means a lot."*

---

* Cynicism check: If you find yourself thinking something like, "The kindest thing I've noticed is that they do their jobs and leave me alone," stop for a second. I'm generally in favor of a witty retort, but notice if your first thought *feels* spiteful or too sharp—it may be a sign of cynicism's alluring pull. Resist! It's okay to notice and offer yourself kindness. And it's a delightfully human thing to do.

4. **"How would you like to feel about how we interact?"**

    - Remember a time when a project or meeting went **well**? Describe what was happening.
    - Describe it and capture the big ideas of what felt good about it.
        » *"The whole team was excited, even though some of us were nervous, too. We had a clear plan and were really interested in starting something new."*

    - Remember a time when a project or a meeting went **poorly**? Describe what was happening.
    - Describe it and capture the big themes of what didn't work.
        » *"It felt like we were being put on the spot for losing a contract we had no control over. Nothing was resolved and we just couldn't find a way to make it work. The apathy was exhausting."*

    - As we work together, let's strive for more of what went well and feels good (often the three Key Behaviors), and let's stop and correct our actions as we're re-creating what went poorly (often jackass behavior).
    - When things are going well or going poorly, what's the kindest, clearest way to notice it?
        » *"Hey this meeting went really well. Thanks for being willing to share your thoughts constructively."*

    - What will we do to acknowledge the good and the bad and make changes as needed?
        » *"Okay, well, that experiment taught us that we **never** want to do anything like it again. Let's do an after-action review and see what we did well and what we need to watch for in the future. Let's learn from this and carry on."*

Can you imagine if the people you worked with could ask, answer, and then follow through on these questions? It's pretty amazing when it happens. You just have to start—and then... practice.

Next Steps

Wondering what to do now that you've complete The Working With Humans Workbook? Here are a few suggestions for your next steps:

What You Can Do Next:

- Review and revisit the exercises. Finish them if you skipped a few while reading.
- Do the Practice with a Pal exercises with many pals.
- Share Working With Humans and this workbook with your team. (They make great gifts.)
- Talk about it with your friends.
- And practice, practice, practice!

Go to *workingwithhumans.com* for more information on how you can keep building all the skills you've been exploring in this book.

Here's to you, your humanity, and the great art of Working With Humans.

A million thanks,
Laura

Ideas to Clarify

Notes and Reflections

About the Author

Laura Crandall founded her management consulting firm, Slate Communication, in 2009. For over thirty years, she has worked in and consulted with industries that include manufacturing, journalism, hospitality, and academia; fifteen of those years were spent managing teams. Laura's work is dedicated to helping people within organizations discover and develop foundational management and communication skills—the things we assume everyone has, but rarely discuss. She is an instructor in the Career and Academic Resource Center at Harvard Extension School, where she teaches about workplace communication. Laura earned her master's degree from Harvard Graduate School of Education, where she studied cognitive neuroscience and organizational behavior.

A Midwesterner at heart, Laura makes her home among the people of New England. Her favorite date of the year is March 4th—the best day to start new endeavors because it is both a date and an imperative command: March Forth! You can connect with her via her website: *LauraCrandall.com*.

Additional Resources

- **Management Models and Organizational Behavior**
- **Emotional and Mental Health**
- **Interesting Things About Cognitive Neuroscience**
- **Good Human Resources Information**

For links to the above topics and other tools for *Working With Humans*, please go to workingwithhumans.com